WOK & STIR-FRY

C·O·O·K·I·N·G
Exciting Ideas for Delicious Meals

Photography by Peter Barry
Designed by Richard Hawke and Claire Leighton
Edited by Jillian Stewart and Kate Cranshaw
Recipes by Judith Ferguson, Lalita Ahmed and
   Carolyn Garner

3447
This edition published 1996 by Bramley Books
© Bramley Books, Godalming, Surrey
All rights reserved
Printed and bound in Hong Kong
ISBN 1-85833-532-9

WOK & STIR-FRY
C·O·O·K·I·N·G
Exciting Ideas for Delicious Meals

Bramley Books

Contents

Introduction

The widespread popularity of Oriental cuisine has led to a great surge in the use of woks in this country. Although the wok is the traditional cooking utensil of the Chinese, it is an extremely versatile piece of kitchen equipment which can be used for deep-frying, boiling, steaming and braising, as well as stir-frying.

Woks vary in the material that they are made of, as well as in size and shape. The basic traditional wok is made of heavy gauge carbon steel and needs to be kept oiled when not in use, as it tends to rust. Aluminium, stainless steel and even non-stick woks are available and are better for steaming, braising or boiling. The shape of a wok is important as it is determined by the type of heat source that is to be used. For example, a round bottomed wok, with a ring-base stand for stability, is for use on gas burners, while a flat bottomed wok is for use on electric rings or halogen hobs.

The cooking method most closely associated with the wok is stir-frying. This is an extremely rapid way of cooking and one which is unique to the wok. The secret of successful stir-frying is to have all the ingredients prepared before you start to cook and to ensure that they are cut finely enough to cook quickly. Meat should be cut into thin slivers or strips and is normally one of the first ingredients in the wok along with the toughest vegetables, such as onions and peppers, as these need slightly longer cooking than softer vegetables. The best oil to use for stir-frying is a vegetable oil such as sunflower or peanut oil (also known as groundnut oil), and always remember to heat the wok thoroughly before the oil is added. Olive oil, butter or margarine are not suitable for stir-frying as these fats are for use at lower temperatures only and will burn if subjected to the intense heat of a wok.

When deep-frying in a wok there are a number of guidelines to follow: make absolutely sure that it is stable before you add the oil; do not put too much oil in the wok, and only start to heat it once the oil has been added; do not over-heat the oil and, to ensure that the correct temperature has been reached, it is best to use a deep-fat frying thermometer. It is also important not to overcrowd the wok, so only add a few of the items to be fried at any one time.

Ingredients are crucial to the end result; vegetables should be as fresh as possible and meat should be of a tender cut that is easy to slice and not fatty. For Chinese recipes, authentic ingredients are necessary to obtain the best results and thankfully many Oriental ingredients are now available in large supermarkets. Cooking with a wok is a quick and satisfying method of preparing meals, and by following these simple guidelines, mastering the art of wok and stir-fry cooking is well within the reach of cooks of all abilities.

SPRING ROLLS

One of the most popular Chinese hors d'oeuvres, these are delicious dipped in sweet-sour sauce or plum sauce.

MAKES 12

Wrappers
120g/4oz strong plain flour
1 egg, beaten
Cold water

Filling
225g/8oz pork, trimmed and finely
    shredded
120g/4oz prawns, peeled and chopped
4 spring onions, finely chopped
2 tsps chopped fresh ginger
120g/4oz Chinese leaves, shredded
100g/3½oz bean sprouts
1 tbsp light soy sauce
Dash sesame seed oil
1 egg, beaten

Oil for deep frying

1. To prepare the wrappers, sift the flour into a bowl and make a well in the centre. Add the beaten egg and about 1 tbsp cold water. Begin beating with a wooden spoon, gradually drawing in the flour from the outside to make a smooth dough. Add more water if necessary.

2. Knead the dough until it is elastic and pliable. Place in a covered bowl and chill for about 4 hours or overnight.

3. When ready to roll out, allow the dough to come back to room temperature. Flour a large work surface well and roll the dough out to about 5mm/¼-inch thick.

4. Cut the dough into 12 equal squares and then roll each piece into a larger square about 15cm/6 inches. The dough should be very thin. Cover with a damp cloth while preparing the filling.

5. Cook the pork in a little of the frying oil for about 2-3 minutes. Add the remaining filling ingredients, except the beaten egg, cook for a further 2-3 minutes and allow to cool.

6. Lay out the wrappers on a clean work surface with a point of each wrapper facing you. Brush the edges lightly with the beaten egg.

7. Divide the filling among all 12 wrappers, placing it just above the front point. Fold over the sides like an envelope.

8. Then fold over the nearest point until the filling is completely covered. Roll up as for a Swiss roll. Press all the edges to seal well.

9. Heat some oil in a wok to 190°C/375°F. Depending upon the size of the fryer, place in 2-4 spring rolls and fry until golden brown on both sides. The rolls will float to the surface when one side has browned and should be turned over. Drain thoroughly on kitchen paper and serve hot.

TIME: Preparation takes about 50 minutes for the wrapper dough, the filling and for rolling up. Dough must be allowed to rest for at least 4 hours before use. Cooking takes about 20 minutes.

SERVING IDEAS: Serve with a dipping sauce. Sweet and sour sauce or hot mustard sauce are available bottled from speciality shops and Chinese supermarkets.

SESAME CHICKEN WINGS

This is an economical starter that is also good as a cocktail snack or as a light meal with stir-fried vegetables.

SERVES 8

12 chicken wings
1 tbsp salted black beans
1 tbsp water
1 tbsp oil
2 cloves garlic, crushed
2 slices fresh ginger, cut into fine shreds
3 tbsps soy sauce
1½ tbsps dry sherry or rice wine
Large pinch black pepper
1 tbsp sesame seeds
Spring onions or coriander leaves to
    garnish

1. Cut off and discard the chicken wing tips. Cut between the joint to separate the wings into two pieces.

2. Crush the beans and add the water. Leave to stand.

3. Heat the oil in a wok and add the garlic and ginger. Stir briefly and add the chicken wings. Cook, stirring, until lightly browned, about 3 minutes. Add the soy sauce and wine and cook, stirring, about 30 seconds longer. Add the soaked black beans and pepper.

4. Cover the wok tightly and allow to simmer for about 8-10 minutes. Uncover and turn the heat to high. Continue cooking, stirring until the liquid is almost evaporated and the chicken wings are glazed with sauce.

5. Remove from the heat and sprinkle on sesame seeds. Stir to coat completely and serve. Garnish with spring onions or coriander if wished.

TIME: Preparation takes about 25 minutes, cooking takes about 13-14 minutes.

WATCHPOINT: Sesame seeds pop slightly as they cook.

COOK'S TIP: You can prepare the chicken wings ahead of time and reheat them. They are best reheated in the oven for about 5 minutes at 180°C/350°F/Gas Mark 4.

SERVING IDEAS: To garnish with spring onion brushes, trim the roots and green tops of spring onions and cut both ends into thin strips, leaving the middle intact. Place in ice water for several hours or overnight for the cut ends to curl up. Drain and use to garnish.

CHEESE NIBBLES

These make delicious snacks as well as starters. Cheese on toast will never be the same again!

MAKES 40

30g/1oz plain flour
1 tsp baking powder
1 tsp dry English mustard
Salt and pepper
60g/2oz Gruyère cheese
60g/2oz Emmental cheese
1 egg, lightly beaten
2 tbsps milk
1 clove garlic, crushed
10 slices stale brown bread
Oil for deep frying

---

1. Sift together the flour, baking powder, mustard, and a pinch of salt and pepper. Grate the cheeses.

2. Mix together cheese, egg, milk, garlic and flour mixture. Beat together well.

3. Trim off bread-crusts, and cut each slice diagonally into 4 triangles.

4. Spread one heaped teaspoon of mixture on each triangle of bread to cover well.

5. Heat some oil in a wok for deep frying. When hot (about 180°C/350°F) carefully fry in batches with bread side up first. Deep fry for 4-5 minutes or until golden brown on both sides.

6. Remove and drain on kitchen paper. Keep hot until all frying is completed. Serve hot.

TIME: Preparation takes 20 minutes and cooking takes about 4-5 minutes per batch.

PREPARATION: Use white bread instead of brown if wished.

VARIATIONS: Use this recipe for conventional cheese on toast and grill instead of deep frying.

CHICKEN AND ASPARAGUS SOUP

This simple soup is based on good chicken stock.

SERVES 4

450g/1lb chicken pieces
1 onion, roughly chopped
1 carrot, roughly chopped
1 celery stick, roughly chopped
4 peppercorns
1 litre/1¾ pints water
Salt and pepper
275g/10oz can asparagus pieces
Chopped parsley to garnish

1. Remove the chicken meat from bones and cut into fine shreds.

2. Put the chicken bones, onion, carrot, celery, peppercorns and water in wok, and season with salt and pepper. Bring to the boil, reduce heat, and simmer for 30 minutes. Strain and return stock to the wok.

3. Add the shredded chicken, and simmer until chicken is cooked. Add undrained asparagus pieces. Adjust seasoning. Serve sprinkled with chopped parsley.

TIME: Prepration takes 10 minutes and cooking takes 45 minutes.

BUYING GUIDE: Use the cheaper pieces of chicken, such as thighs, for this dish.

VARIATIONS: Use flat leaf parsley or coriander leaves to float on the surface of the soup as a garnish.

EGGFLOWER SOUP

This is a good soup to make at short notice as it is quick to prepare and uses ingredients that you are likely to have to hand.

SERVES 4

400g/14oz can plum tomatoes
1 tbsp light soy sauce
570ml/1 pint chicken stock
2 spring onions, finely chopped
2 eggs, lightly beaten

1. Drain and chop the tomatoes, removing pips, and reserve juice. Bring soy sauce, tomato juice and stock to the boil in a wok.

2. Add the tomatoes and half the spring onions, and cook for 2 minutes.

3. Dribble the beaten eggs in gradually, stirring continuously. Serve immediately, sprinkled with the remaining spring onions.

TIME: Preparation takes 10 minutes and cooking takes about 10 minutes.

VARIATIONS: Use a little parsley or a few chives instead of the spring onions.

PREPARATION: The quickest way to remove the tomato pips is to cut them in half and use a teaspoon to scoop them out.

PRAWN TOAST

These little toasts make delicious finger food for parties.

MAKES 20

225g/8oz prawns peeled and de-veined,
    and chopped finely
1 small egg, beaten
2 tsps sherry
2 tsps oyster sauce
½ tsp grated fresh root ginger
2 tsp cornflour
Salt
5 slices white bread
Oil for deep frying

1. Combine the prawns, beaten egg, sherry, oyster sauce, grated ginger, cornflour and a pinch of salt.

2. Using a 4cm/1½ inch round pastry cutter, cut out 20 circles of bread.

3. Spread some of the prawn mixture on each piece of bread to cover well.

4. Heat enough oil in a wok for deep frying. Fry in batches with bread side up first, until bread is golden brown.

5. Remove and drain on kitchen paper. Keep hot until all frying is completed.

TIME: Preparation takes 15 minutes and cooking takes about 4-5 minutes per batch.

VARIATIONS: Cut the bread into other, similar sized shapes such as squares or triangles.

SERVING IDEAS: Serve with a chilli sauce or spicy tomato sauce for dipping.

DEEP-FRIED CHICKEN WITH LEMON SLICES

This exciting dish has quite a few ingredients, but it is well worth the effort.

SERVES 6

1.4kg/3lbs chicken breast meat
90g/3oz cornflour
3 tbsps plain flour
1 green pepper
1 red pepper
Oil for deep frying

Marinade
½ tsp salt
½ tbsp cooking wine
½ tbsp light soy sauce
1 tbsp cornflour
1 tbsp water
1 egg yolk
Black pepper

Sauce
3 tbsps sugar
3 tbsps lemon juice
90ml/6 tbsps light stock
½ tsp salt
2 tbsps cornflour
1 tsp sesame oil

2 lemons to garnish, thinly sliced
Chopped parsley to garnish

1. Skin the chicken. Cut into bite-sized, thin slices.

2. Mix all the marinade ingredients together and marinate the chicken in the mixture for 10 minutes.

3. Mix the cornflour and plain flour together on a plate, remove the chicken from the marinade and coat each chicken piece with the flour mixture.

4. Mix all the sauce ingredients together in a small bowl. Cut the peppers into 2.5cm/ 1-inch pieces.

5. Place a 12-inch wok over a high heat. Heat the oil until almost smoking. Deep-fry the chicken slices until golden brown. Remove with a slotted spoon to a heated plate. Pour off all but 1 tbsp of the oil.

6. Stir-fry the pepper until it begins to brown. Pour in the sauce and bring to the boil, stirring until thickened. Add the chicken pieces. Stir for a further few minutes.

7. Transfer to a heated serving platter, and garnish with lemon slices and chopped parsley.

TIME: Preparation takes 30 minutes, cooking takes about 15 minutes.

BUYING GUIDE: If you have a freezer, stock up on the economy-sized bags of half-boned chicken and bone it yourself to save on the cost of fresh breast meat.

QUICK FRIED PRAWNS

*Prepared with either raw or cooked prawns, this incredibly delicious dish
is extremely easy to cook.*

SERVES 4

900g/2lbs cooked prawns in their shells
2 cloves garlic, crushed
2.5cm/1-inch piece fresh root ginger, finely
　　chopped
1 tbsp chopped fresh coriander
3 tbsps oil
1 tbsp rice wine or dry sherry
1½ tbsps light soy sauce
Chopped spring onions to garnish

1. Shell the prawns except for the very tail ends. Place the prawns in a bowl with the remaining ingredients, except for the garnish, and leave to marinate for 30 minutes.

2. Heat the wok and add the prawns and their marinade. Stir-fry briefly to heat the prawns.

3. Chop the spring onions roughly or cut into neat rounds. Sprinkle over the prawns to serve.

TIME: Preparation takes about 30 minutes for the prawns to marinate.
Cooking takes about 2 minutes.

WATCHPOINT: Do not overcook the prawns as they will toughen.

VARIATIONS: If uncooked prawns are available, stir-fry with their marinade
until they turn pink.

SEAFOOD COMBINATION

If you don't like squid make up the weight with more prawns or fish.

SERVES 4

1 tbsp dry white wine
½ tsp salt
1 egg white
1 tsp grated fresh root ginger
1 tsp cornflour
225g/8oz prawns, peeled and de-veined
120g/4oz white fish fillets, cut into 2.5cm/
    1-inch cubes
120g/4oz squid, cleaned, cut into 2.5cm/
    1-inch rings, opened up, and scored with
    lattice design
120g/4oz mange tout, trimmed
Oil for deep frying
1 carrot, cut into matchstick strips
1 celery stick, sliced diagonally

1. Combine the wine, salt, egg white, grated ginger and cornflour, and mix well.

2. Add the prawns and fish, and toss well. Drain prawns and fish, reserving sauce.

3. Blanch mange tout in boiling water for 1 minute. Drain.

4. Heat the oil in a wok. Deep fry prawns, fish and squid for 2 minutes. Remove from the pan and drain on kitchen paper.

5. Carefully remove the oil from the wok, reserving 1 tbsp of oil in the wok. Heat oil. Stir-fry carrot and celery for 3 minutes.

6. Add mange tout and stir-fry a further 3 minutes. Add any remaining sauce and stir.

7. Add the seafood and toss well until heated through.

TIME: Preparation takes 20 minutes and cooking about 20 minutes.

COOK'S TIP: Scoring the squid helps to tenderise it.

BUYING GUIDE: Choose a firm-fleshed white fish for this dish – monkfish and cod are particularly good.

STIR-FRIED SALAD

Stir-fries are served hot, but the ingredients are cooked so quickly that they retain all of their crunchiness.

SERVES 4

1 onion
2 large leeks
60ml/4 tbsps olive oil
2 cloves garlic, crushed
225g/8oz mange tout peas, topped and
    tailed
120g/4oz bean sprouts, or lentil sprouts
Salt and freshly ground black pepper
1 tbsp fresh chopped coriander leaf

1. Cut the onion into thin rings.
2. Trim the leeks and cut each down the length of one side. Open the leeks out and wash thoroughly under running water.

3. Cut each leek into 3 pieces, then thinly slice each piece lengthways into thin strips.

4. Heat the oil in a large wok and add the onions and garlic. Cook for 2 minutes, stirring all the time, until the onions have softened but not browned.

5. Add the mange tout and sliced leeks to the wok and continue stir-frying for 4 minutes.

6. Add the remaining ingredients and cook briskly for a further 2 minutes. Serve piping hot.

TIME: Preparation takes 15 minutes, cooking takes approximately 10 minutes.

COOK'S TIP: Sprout your own beans or lentils by putting them into a glass jar, rinse thoroughly and pour in fresh water each day, cover with muslin, and stand the jar on a sunny windowsill. After 3-4 days, the beans or lentils will have sprouted.

SERVING IDEAS: Serve this dish with rice, and sprinkle it liberally with soy sauce.

LAMB MEATBALLS WITH YOGURT

This dish turns humble mince into an exotic treat.

SERVES 4

450g/1lb lean minced lamb
2 cloves garlic, crushed
1 small onion, grated
½ tsp chilli powder
1 tsp garam masala
1 tbsp chopped mint
30g/1oz breadcrumbs
1 egg, lightly beaten
Salt and pepper
2 tbsps oil
Small pinch of saffron strands, or ¼ tsp
    ground turmeric
2 tbsps boiling water
75ml/5 tbsps natural yogurt
Fresh coriander or mint to garnish

1. In a bowl, mix together the minced lamb, garlic, onion, chilli powder, garam masala, mint and breadcrumbs.

2. Add lightly beaten egg to bind ingredients together and salt and pepper to taste.

3. Wet hands. Take a teaspoon of mixture, and roll between palms, forming small balls.

4. Heat a wok and add the oil. Add the meatballs, shake wok to make meatballs roll around, and fry until browned well all over.

5. Add the saffron or turmeric to 2 tbsps boiling water. Leave to stand for 5 minutes.

6. Add the saffron water to yogurt, and stir in until evenly mixed.

7. Reheat meatballs and serve on a pool of yogurt. Garnish with fresh mint or coriander.

TIME: Preparation takes 15 minutes and cooking takes about 30 minutes.

VARIATIONS: Substitute lean minced pork for the lamb.

SERVING IDEAS: Serve with boiled rice and pitta bread.

PORK SPARERIBS WITH CHINESE MUSHROOMS

Spareribs served with Chinese mushrooms in a slightly hot and spicy sauce.

SERVES 4

900g/2lbs pork spareribs
1 carrot, finely sliced
1 leek, finely chopped
1 bay leaf
175g/6oz dried Chinese mushrooms,
    soaked for 15 minutes in warm water
    and drained
1 tbsp oil
1 tsp chopped garlic
½ tsp chilli sauce
1 tbsp soy sauce
1 tbsp hoisin sauce
1 tsp wine vinegar
280ml/½ pint chicken stock
Salt and pepper

---

1. Cut the spareribs down the bone to separate them. Now cut them into smaller pieces, so that they are easier to handle. In a medium-sized, flameproof casserole bring to the boil plenty of water along with the carrot, leek and bay leaf. Blanch the spareribs for 1 minute in the boiling water. Remove and drain well.

2. Cook the mushrooms in the boiling water for 10 minutes. Drain well, discarding the water.

3. Heat the oil in a wok, add the garlic, chilli sauce and the mushrooms. Fry slowly until lightly coloured.

4. Stir in the soy sauce, hoisin sauce, vinegar and stock.

5. Add the spareribs, stirring all the ingredients together well. Season with salt and pepper to taste and cook, covered, for 10 minutes.

6. Remove the lid and allow the sauce to reduce slightly. Serve piping hot.

TIME: Preparation takes about 15 minutes, soaking the mushrooms about 15 minutes and cooking takes approximately 20 minutes.

VARIATIONS: If you cannot buy hoisin sauce, replace it with 1 tsp sugar.

WATCHPOINT: You should not blanch the spareribs for longer than 1 minute.

SPICED LAMB

Tender sautéed lamb is delicious in a sauce that's fragrant with herbs and spices.

SERVES 4

450g/1lb lamb neck fillet
1 tsp fresh dill, chopped
1 tsp rosemary, crushed
1 tsp fresh thyme, chopped
2 tsp mustard seeds, slightly crushed
2 bay leaves
1 tsp coarsely ground black pepper
½ tsp ground allspice
Juice 2 lemons
280ml/½ pint red wine
2 tbsps oil
1 small red pepper, sliced
90g/3oz button mushrooms, left whole
30g/1oz butter or margarine
3 tbsps flour
140ml/¼ pint beef stock
Salt

1. Place the lamb in a shallow dish and sprinkle on the dill, rosemary, thyme and mustard seeds. Add the bay leaves, pepper, allspice, lemon juice and wine, and stir to coat the meat thoroughly with the marinade. Leave for 4 hours in the refrigerator.

2. Heat the oil in a large wok and add the red pepper and mushrooms and cook to soften slightly. Remove with a draining spoon.

3. Reheat the oil in the pan and add the lamb fillet, well drained and patted dry. Reserve marinade. Brown meat quickly on all sides to seal. Remove from the wok and set aside with the vegetables.

4. Melt the butter in the wok and when foaming add the flour. Lower the heat and cook the flour slowly until a good, rich brown. Pour in the beef stock and the marinade. Bring to the boil and return the vegetables and lamb to the pan. Cook about 12-15 minutes, or until the lamb is tender, but still pink inside.

5. Slice the lamb fillet thinly on the diagonal and arrange on plates. Remove the bay leaves from the sauce and spoon over the meat to serve.

TIME: Preparation takes about 25 minutes, plus 4 hours marinating time for the meat. Cooking takes about 25 minutes.

VARIATIONS: This recipe can be prepared with pork fillet or steak but ensure the meat is cooked through and not pink in the centre.

SERVING IDEAS: Serve with rice or sauté potatoes.

STEAMED FISH ROLLS

Rolled fish looks elegant and makes a dish that is slightly out of the ordinary.

SERVES 4

2 large sole or plaice, cut into 4 fillets
175g/6oz peeled prawns, chopped
2 tsps cornflour
1 tsp dry sherry
4 spring onions, green part only, chopped
2 eggs, beaten with a pinch of salt

1. Lay the fillets skin side down, with the tail end nearest you. Keeping a sharp knife at a 45° angle, cut away from you using a sawing action, whilst holding onto the skin and pulling it towards you as the flesh comes free. Roll the flesh away as you cut. Place the fillets skinned-side up on a flat surface.

2. Mix the prawns with the cornflour, sherry and spring onions. Divide this mixture equally between the plaice fillets.

3. Cook the eggs in a wok, stirring continuously until they are softly scrambled. Spread equal quantities of this over the prawn mixture.

4. Roll up the fish fillets swiss roll fashion, starting from the thicker end. Secure with wooden cocktail sticks.

5. Put the fish rolls on a wire rack over the wok and fill the bottom with boiling water. Cover and steam for 10-15 minutes over a medium heat, until the fish is cooked. Remove the cocktail sticks and serve immediately.

TIME: Preparation takes 25 minutes and cooking takes 10-15 minutes.

SERVING IDEAS: Serve with new potatoes and a fresh mixed salad.

PREPARATION: Use a little salt to help keep hold of the fish skin when preparing the fillets. Keeping the knife angled downwards, towards the skin prevents the blade from cutting the flesh of the fish.

COOK'S TIP: Spread more of the filling towards the thicker end of the fillets to help prevent it falling out as you roll.

Mange Tout with Prawns

Mange tout peas are delicious and should be cooked so that they still have a slight crunch.

SERVES 2-4

3 tbsps oil
60g/2oz split blanched almonds, halved
120g/4oz mange tout
2 tsps cornflour
2 tsps light soy sauce
175ml/6 fl oz chicken stock
30ml/2 tbsps dry sherry
Salt and pepper
450g/1lb cooked, peeled prawns
60g/2oz bamboo shoots, sliced

1. Heat the oil in a wok. Add the almonds and cook over moderate heat until golden brown. Remove from the oil and drain on kitchen paper.

2. To prepare the mange tout, tear off the stems and pull them downwards to remove any strings. If the mange tout are small, just remove the stalks.

3. Add the mange tout to the hot oil and cook for about 1 minute. Remove and set aside with the almonds.

4. Drain all the oil from the wok and mix together the cornflour and the remaining ingredients, except the prawns and bamboo shoots.

5. Pour the mixture into the wok and stir constantly while bringing to the boil. Allow to simmer for 1-2 minutes until thickened and cleared.

6. Stir in the prawns and all the other ingredients and heat through for about 1 minute. Serve immediately.

TIME: Preparation takes about 10 minutes, cooking takes 6-8 minutes.

VARIATIONS: If using spring onions, celery or water chestnuts, cook with the mange tout.

WATCHPOINT: Do not cook the prawns too long or on heat that is too high – they toughen quite easily.

BEEF WITH PINEAPPLE AND PEPPERS

Cutting steak into thin strips helps the marinade flavour to penetrate the meat and ensures that cooking is brief.

SERVES 4

2 tbsps light soy sauce
1 tsp sugar
2 tsps cornflour
2 tbsps water
450g/1lb fillet or rump steak, sliced thinly
1 tbsp peanut oil
1 tsp chopped fresh root ginger
2 cloves garlic, crushed
1 onion, roughly chopped
1 green pepper, roughly chopped
1 red pepper, roughly chopped
1 can pineapple slices, drained and
   chopped

Sauce
1 tbsp plum sauce
1 tbsp dark soy sauce
1 tsp sugar
1 tsp sesame oil
1 tsp cornflour
60ml/4 tbsps water
Salt and pepper

1. Combine the light soy sauce with the sugar, cornflour and water. Mix well and pour over steak. Toss together well, and put aside for at least 30 minutes, turning occasionally.

2. Heat a wok and add the peanut oil. Add the ginger, garlic, onion and peppers, and stir-fry for 3 minutes. Remove from the wok and set aside.

3. Add extra oil if necessary, and stir-fry the beef, well separated, for 2 minutes. Remove from the wok.

4. Mix together all sauce ingredients in the wok, and heat until the sauce begins to thicken.

5. Add the vegetables, beef and pineapple, and toss together over a high heat until heated through.

TIME: Preparation takes about 40 minutes, including marinating. Cooking takes 15 minutes.

COOK'S TIP: If you partially freeze the steak, it makes it a lot easier to slice thinly.

SERVING IDEAS: Serve with boiled rice.

PORK WITH CHILLI

Use an amount of chilli that suits yourself. Remember that the smaller the chilli the hotter it is.

SERVES 4

1 clove garlic, crushed

1 tsp sugar

1 tsp peanut oil

1 tsp Chinese wine, or dry sherry

1 tsp cornflour

275g/10oz lean pork fillet, cut into 2.5cm/
   1-inch cubes

140ml/¼ pint peanut oil, for deep frying

1 green pepper, sliced

1 red chilli, seeds removed, and sliced
   finely

4 spring onions, chopped

Sauce

1 tsp chilli powder

2 tbsps dark soy sauce

1 tsp Worcestershire sauce

½ tsp five-spice powder

Pinch of salt

1. Mix together the garlic, sugar, 1 tsp peanut oil, wine and cornflour, and pour over the pork. Cover and leave to marinate for at least 1 hour, turning occasionally.

2. Meanwhile, combine the ingredients for the sauce in a bowl. Mix well. Set aside.

3. Heat the oil for deep frying in a wok until hot. Toss in the pork cubes, and cook for about 10 minutes, or until golden brown and cooked through. Drain and set aside.

4. Carefully remove all but 1 tbsp of oil from the wok. Heat the oil and add the green pepper, chilli and spring onions. Stir-fry for 2 minutes.

5. Add the sauce and pork to the wok, and bring to the boil, stirring continuously. Adjust the seasoning and serve immediately.

TIME: Preparation takes 1 hour, including marinating. Cooking takes about 15 minutes.

WATCHPOINT: Allow oil to cool before removing from the wok.

SERVING IDEAS: Serve with egg fried rice or noodles.

STIR-FRY TOFU SALAD

Ideal for vegetarians, but so delicious that it will be enjoyed by everyone.

SERVES 4-6

1 block of tofu
120g/4oz mange tout
60g/2oz mushrooms
2 carrots, peeled
2 celery sticks
4 spring onions
140ml/¼ pint vegetable oil
60g/2oz broccoli florets
3 tbsps lemon juice
2 tsps honey
1 tsp grated fresh ginger
3 tbsps soy sauce
Dash of sesame oil
60g/2oz unsalted roasted peanuts
120g/4oz bean sprouts
½ head Chinese leaves

1. Drain the tofu well and press gently to remove any excess moisture. Cut into 1.25cm/½-inch cubes.

2. Trim the tops and tails from the mange tout peas.

3. Thinly slice the mushrooms with a sharp knife.

4. Cut the carrots and celery into thin slices, on the diagonal.

5. Trim the spring onions and slice them in the same way as the carrots and celery.

6. Heat 2 tbsps of the vegetable oil in a wok or large frying pan. Stir in the mange tout, mushrooms, celery, carrots and broccoli, and cook for 2 minutes, stirring constantly.

7. Remove the vegetables from the wok and set them aside to cool.

8. Put the remaining oil into a small bowl and whisk in the lemon juice, honey, ginger, soy sauce and sesame oil.

9. Stir the sliced spring onions, peanuts and bean sprouts into the cooled vegetables.

10. Mix the dressing into the salad vegetables, then add the tofu. Toss the tofu into the salad very carefully so that it does not break up.

11. Shred the Chinese leaves and arrange them on a serving platter. Pile the salad ingredients over the top and serve well-chilled.

TIME: Preparation takes approximately 25 minutes, cooking takes 2-4 minutes.

PREPARATION: Make sure that the stir-fried vegetables are completely cool before adding the remaining salad ingredients, or they will lose their crispness.

VARIATIONS: Shredded cooked chicken can be used in place of the tofu in this recipe, for a non-vegetarian dish.

GINGER SCALLOPS IN OYSTER SAUCE

Scallops have a lovely delicate flavour and are prized in many cuisines, especially Cantonese.

SERVES 4

450g/1lb scallops, cleaned, dried on kitchen paper, and sliced
Salt
2 tbsps vegetable oil
2.5cm/1-inch fresh root ginger, peeled and very thinly sliced
10 spring onions, sliced diagonally into 2.5cm/1-inch slices

Sauce
1 tbsp oyster sauce
1 tbsp light soy sauce
½ tsp sesame oil
1 tsp cornflour
Pinch of sugar
1 tsp grated fresh root ginger
75ml/5 tbsps light chicken stock

1. Combine oyster sauce, soy sauce, sesame oil, cornflour, sugar and grated ginger and set aside.

2. Sprinkle the scallops with a pinch of salt.

3. Heat a wok, and add the oil. Add sliced ginger and spring onions, and stir-fry gently for 1 minute.

4. Raise heat to high. Add scallops and stir-fry for 1 minute.

5. Add the sauce mixture and stir in. Remove from heat, and stir in stock gradually.

6. Return to heat and bring to the boil, stirring continuously.

7. Simmer gently for 3 minutes, until sauce is slightly thickened.

8. Adjust seasoning, serve immediately.

TIME: Preparation takes about 10 minutes and cooking takes about 15 minutes.

WATCHPOINT: Do not over cook the scallops.

BUYING GUIDE: Scallops can also be bought frozen, but make sure they are totally defrosted before cooking them.

STIR-FRIED LEEKS AND LAMB

Rosemary, redcurrant jelly and mint are all classic accompaniments to lamb and complement it perfectly.

SERVES 4

1 tbsp oil
2 tsps fresh rosemary
2 tsps fresh basil leaves, chopped
450g/1lb leeks, cut into 2.5cm/1-inch slices
450g/1lb lamb, cut into 2.5cm/1-inch cubes
400g/14oz can plum tomatoes
1 tsp redcurrant jelly
1 tbsp chopped mint
Salt and pepper
Fresh mint to garnish

1. Heat a wok and add the oil. Add the rosemary, basil and leeks, and stir-fry gently for 3 minutes. Remove from the wok, and increase the heat.

2. Add the lamb and stir-fry until well-browned all over.

3. Return the leeks to the wok. Add the undrained tomatoes, redcurrant jelly, mint, and salt and pepper to taste.

4. Cover and simmer for 20 minutes, adding water if necessary. Serve hot, garnished with fresh mint.

TIME: Preparation takes about 10 minutes and cooking takes 30 minutes.

PREPARATION: If fresh basil and rosemary are unavailable, use dried herbs but half the quantity as the flavour is stronger.

VARIATIONS: Try using cooked lamb but adjust the cooking time accordingly.

BEEF WITH MANGO

This combination of beef with mango is delicious.

SERVES 4

1 can mango slices, drained, reserving
   60ml/4 tbsps mango juice
1 tsp sugar
1 tsp cornflour
½ tsp salt
Pinch of pepper
450g/1lb fillet or rump steak, thinly sliced
2 tbsps mango chutney
1 tbsp plum sauce
1 tbsp oil

1. Combine 2 tbsps of the mango juice, with the sugar, cornflour, salt and pepper, and pour over the sliced steak. Toss well and set aside for 15 minutes.

2. Mix remaining mango juice with the mango chutney and plum sauce, and set aside.

3. Finely chop half of the mangoes and add to the sauce, retaining enough slices for decoration.

4. Heat a wok and add the oil.

5. Stir-fry steak for 5 minutes, tossing well, or until browned all over.

6. Add the mango-plum sauce and cook for a further 5 minutes.

7. Garnish dish with reserved mango slices.

TIME: Preparation takes about 20 minutes, including marinating. Cooking takes about 10 minutes.

PREPARATION: Partially freeze the meat before slicing as this will make it much easier to cut the meat thinly.

SERVING IDEAS: Serve with rice, garnished with spring onion flowers.

PRAWN AND SCALLOP STIR-FRY

Pine nuts and spinach give an unusual twist to this delicious dish.

SERVES 4

3 tbsps oil
60g/4 tbsps pine nuts
450g/1lb uncooked prawns, peeled
450g/1lb shelled scallops, quartered if large
2 tsps grated fresh ginger
1 small red or green chilli, seeded and
    finely chopped
2 cloves garlic, finely chopped
1 large red pepper, cut into 2.5cm/1-inch
    diagonal pieces
225g/8oz fresh spinach, stalks removed and
    leaves well washed and shredded
4 spring onions, cut in 1.5cm/½-inch
    diagonal pieces
60ml/4 tbsps fish or chicken stock
60ml/4 tbsps light soy sauce
60ml/4 tbsps rice wine or dry sherry
1 tbsp cornflour

1. Heat oil in a wok and add the pine nuts. Cook over low heat, stirring continuously until lightly browned. Remove with a draining spoon and drain on kitchen paper.

2. Add the prawns and scallops to the oil remaining the wok and stir over moderate heat until shellfish is beginning to look opaque and firm, and the prawns look pink.

3. Add the ginger, chilli, garlic and red pepper and cook a few minutes over moderately high heat.

4. Add the spinach and onion, and stir-fry briefly. Mix the remaining ingredients together and pour over the ingredients in the wok.

5. Turn up the heat to bring the liquid to the boil, stirring ingredients constantly. Once the liquid thickens and clears, stir in the pine nuts and serve immediately.

TIME: Preparation takes about 35 minutes, cooking takes about 8-10 minutes.

PREPARATION: Because cooking time is so short, be sure to prepare all ingredients and have them ready before beginning to stir-fry.

ECONOMY: Eliminate scallops and cut the quantity of prawns in half. Make up the difference with a firm whitefish cut into 2.5cm/1-inch pieces.

KIDNEYS WITH BACON

Kidneys are highly nutritious but are often cooked unimaginatively, so try
something new with this dish.

SERVES 4

450g/1lb lambs' kidneys
3 tbsps sherry
2 tbsps oil
8 rashers streaky bacon, diced
1 onion, quartered
3 garlic cloves, crushed
1 tbsp tomato chutney
1 tbsp light soy sauce
2 tbsps water
Salt and pepper
1 tbsp cornflour
1 tbsp chopped parsley
Sprig of parsley to garnish

---

1. Cut the kidneys in half and remove hard core with a sharp knife or scissors.

2. Cut a lattice design on back of kidneys. Pour over sherry, and set aside for 15 minutes.

3. Heat a wok and add the oil. Add bacon, onion and garlic, and stir-fry for 5 minutes. Remove from wok.

4. Add the kidneys, reserving sherry, and fry for 3 minutes.

5. Stir in the tomato chutney. Add soy sauce and water to wok, and return bacon and onion mixture. Add salt and pepper to taste. Cover and simmer gently for 10 minutes.

6. Meanwhile, blend the cornflour with the sherry marinade.

7. Add the parsley and cornflour mixture, and stir, cooking gently until sauce thickens. Garnish with parsley.

TIME: Preparation takes about 20 minutes, including 15 minutes marinating.
Cooking takes about 25 minutes.

COOK'S TIP: Do not overcook the kidneys or cook them too fast or they
will become tough.

SERVING IDEAS: Serve immediately with boiled rice.

BEEF AND OYSTER SAUCE

Oyster sauce has a rich, subtle flavour which complements beef perfectly.

SERVES 4

450g/1lb fillet or rump steak, sliced into thin
   strips
2 tbsps light soy sauce
2 tbsps peanut or vegetable oil
2 onions, quartered
2 celery sticks, diagonally sliced
120g/4oz button mushrooms
1 red pepper, roughly chopped
120g/4oz bean sprouts

Oyster Sauce
3 tbsps oyster sauce
½ chicken stock cube dissolved in 2 tbsps
   boiling water
1 tbsp dark soy sauce
1 tbsp Chinese wine or dry sherry
1 tbsp cornflour
2 tbsps cold water
Salt and pepper

1. Place the steak in a bowl and pour over the light soy sauce. Toss together well and set aside for at least 30 minutes.

2. Meanwhile, mix together the oyster sauce, chicken stock, dark soy sauce and wine.

3. Blend together the cornflour and cold water, and set aside.

4. Heat a wok, and add the oil. Add onion, celery, mushrooms and red pepper, and stir-fry for 5 minutes. Remove from wok and set aside.

5. Reheat the oil and, when hot, toss in steak. Brown well all over, then add sauce and fried vegetables.

6. Add the cornflour mixture and bring to the boil, tossing continuously. Add salt and pepper to taste.

7. Finally, add bean sprouts and simmer gently for 3 minutes.

TIME: Preparation takes 35 minutes, including marinating. Cooking takes
20 minutes.

PREPARATION: Partially freezing the beef, before slicing it, makes it easier
to cut thinly.

SERVING IDEAS: Serve with rice or egg noodles.

BRAISED PORK WITH SPINACH AND MUSHROOMS

If available, you could use Chinese greens, such as pak choi instead of spinach.

SERVES 4

4 dried Chinese mushrooms
2 tbsps peanut oil
½ tsp ground nutmeg
225g/8oz spinach leaves, washed and
    shredded, hard stalks removed
1 clove garlic, crushed
1 onion, quartered
Salt
Pepper
1 tbsp flour
450g/1lb lean pork fillet, cut into thin strips
2 tbsps water

1. Soak the mushrooms in hot water for 20 minutes, then discard the stems and finely chop the caps.

2. Heat a wok, add 1 tsp of the oil, and roll it around to coat the surface. Put nutmeg and spinach in wok, and cook gently for 5 minutes. Remove from the wok.

3. Add remaining oil to wok and fry garlic and onion over gentle heat for 5 minutes. Remove from wok.

4. Meanwhile, add a good pinch of salt and freshly-ground black pepper to the flour and toss in the pork, coating well.

5. Fry pork until each piece is browned all over. Add the water and mushrooms, and return onion mixture to wok. Cover and simmer gently for 10 minutes, stirring occasionally.

6. Add spinach and salt and pepper to taste, and cook, uncovered, for 2 minutes.

TIME: Preparation takes 20 minutes and cooking takes about 25 minutes.

BUYING GUIDE: Fresh Chinese shiitake mushrooms are now available in some large supermarkets.

VARIATIONS: Use chicken breast meat in place of pork fillet.

CALVES' LIVER WITH PIQUANT SAUCE

Calves' liver is delicious but quite expensive so you could use lambs' liver as a substitute.

SERVES 4

30g/1oz butter
1 tbsp flour
280ml/½ pint brown or beef stock
1 tbsp tomato purée
1 clove garlic, crushed
1 tsp English mustard
Salt and pepper
2 tbsps tomato, mango, or other fruit
    chutney
450g/1lb calves' liver
1 tbsp oil
1 onion, sliced
Chopped parsley to garnish

1. Heat a wok and add the butter. When melted, stir in flour and cook until lightly browned.

2. Remove from heat and gradually stir in stock. Return to heat and add tomato purée and garlic. Stir until boiling.

3. Add mustard and salt and pepper to taste, and simmer for 5 minutes.

4. Add chutney and mix well. Remove from wok and set aside.

5. Meanwhile, slice liver very thinly. Wash and drain on kitchen paper.

6. Heat the wok and add the oil. When hot add the onion. Fry gently over medium heat until just changing colour.

7. Add slices of liver in a single layer, and fry for about 3 minutes on each side, depending on thickness of slices. The liver should be cooked through and still tender. Do not overcook.

8. Add the piquant sauce to the wok and toss together. Sprinkle with chopped parsley, and serve immediately.

TIME: Preparation takes 10 minutes and cooking 25 minutes.

WATCHPOINT: Do not overcook the liver or it will become tough.

SERVING IDEAS: Serve on a bed of rice and accompany with broccoli.

SQUID WITH BROCCOLI AND CAULIFLOWER

Squid is sweet and tender when cooked and can be prepared in many ways.

SERVES 4

450g/1lb squid, cleaned
140ml/¼ pint oil for deep frying
1 onion, roughly chopped
2 celery sticks, diagonally sliced
225g/8oz fresh broccoli florets
225g/8oz fresh cauliflower florets
½ tsp grated fresh root ginger
1 tbsp cornflour
2 tbsps water
2 tbsps light soy sauce
2 tbsps Chinese wine, or dry sherry
2 tbsps oyster sauce
½ tsp sesame oil
½ tsp sugar
Salt and pepper

1. Cut the cleaned squid lengthways down the centre. Flatten out with inside uppermost. With a sharp knife make a lattice design, cutting deep into the squid flesh.

2. Heat the oil in a wok. Add the squid and cook until it curls. Remove from pan and drain on kitchen paper.

3. Carefully pour off all but 1 tbsp of oil. Add onion, celery, broccoli, cauliflower and ginger, and stir-fry for 3 minutes.

4. Blend the cornflour with the water, and add the soy sauce, wine, oyster sauce, sesame oil, sugar, and salt and pepper to taste. Mix well and add to wok. Bring to the boil and simmer for 3 minutes, stirring continuously.

5. Return the squid to the wok and cook until heated through. Place in a warm serving dish and serve hot.

TIME: Preparation takes 15 minutes and cooking takes about 20 minutes.

COOK'S TIP: Scoring the squid helps to tenderise it and makes it curl when cooking.

BUYING GUIDE: Fresh squid is available most of the year around and can also be bought frozen.

CANTONESE EGG FU YUNG

As the name suggests, this dish is from Canton. However, fu yung dishes are
popular in many other regions of China, too.

SERVES 2-3

5 eggs
60g/2oz shredded cooked meat, poultry or
    fish
1 celery stick, finely shredded
4 Chinese dried mushrooms, soaked in
    boiling water for 5 minutes
60g/2oz bean sprouts
1 small onion, thinly sliced
Pinch salt and pepper
1 tsp dry sherry
Oil for frying

Sauce
1 tbsp cornflour dissolved in 3 tbsps cold
    water
280ml/½ pint chicken stock
1 tsp tomato ketchup
1 tbsp soy sauce
Pinch salt and pepper
Dash sesame oil

1. Beat the eggs lightly and add the shredded meat and celery.

2. Squeeze all the liquid from the dried mushrooms. Remove the stems and cut the caps into thin slices. Add to the egg mixture along with the bean sprouts and onion. Add a pinch of salt and pepper.and the sherry and stir well.

3. Heat a wok or frying pan and pour in about 60ml/4 tbsps oil. When hot, carefully spoon in about 90ml/3 fl oz of the egg mixture.

4. Brown on one side, turn over gently and brown the other side. Remove the cooked patty to a plate and continue until all the mixture is cooked.

5. Combine all the sauce ingredients in a small, heavy-based pan and bring slowly to the boil, stirring continuously until thickened and cleared. Pour the sauce over the Egg Fu Yung to serve.

TIME: Preparation takes 25 minutes, cooking takes about 5 minutes for the
patties and 8 minutes for the sauce.

VARIATIONS: Use cooked shellfish such as crab, prawns or lobster, if
wished. Fresh mushrooms may be used instead of the dried ones. Divide
mixture in half or in thirds and cook one large patty per person.

BEEF WITH BROCCOLI

The traditional Chinese method of cutting meat for stir-frying, used in this recipe,
ensures that the meat will be tender and will cook quickly.

SERVES 2-3

450g/1lb rump steak, partially frozen
60ml/4 tbsps dark soy sauce
1 tbsp cornflour
1 tbsp dry sherry
1 tsp sugar
225g/8oz fresh broccoli
90ml/6 tbsps oil
2.5cm/1-inch piece fresh root ginger,
    peeled and shredded
Salt and pepper

1. Trim any fat from the meat and cut into very thin strips across the grain. Strips should be about 7.5cm/3 inches long.

2. Combine the meat with the soy sauce, cornflour, sherry and sugar. Stir well and leave long enough for the meat to completely defrost.

3. Trim the florets from the stalks of the broccoli and cut them into small even-sized pieces. Peel the stalks off the broccoli and cut into thin, diagonal slices.

4. Heat a wok and add 2 tbsps of the oil to it. Add the broccoli and sprinkle with salt. Stir-fry, turning constantly, until the broccoli is dark green. Do not cook for longer than 2 minutes. Remove from the wok and set aside.

5. Place the remaining oil in the wok and add the ginger and beef. Stir-fry, turning constantly, for about 2 minutes. Return the broccoli to the pan and mix well. Heat through for 30 seconds and serve immediately.

TIME: Preparation takes about 25 minutes and cooking takes about 4 minutes.

PREPARATION: Using meat that is partially frozen makes it easier to get very thin slices.

COOK'S TIP: If more sauce is preferred, double the quantities of soy sauce, cornflour, dry sherry and sugar.

PORK CHOW MEIN

This favourite Chinese meal is quick and simple to prepare, and makes a refreshing change for a midweek lunch or supper.

SERVES 4

275g/10oz egg noodles
1 tbsp Chinese wine, or dry sherry
1 tbsp light soy sauce
1 tsp sugar
450g/1lb pork fillet, thinly sliced
3 tbsps oil
1 tsp grated root ginger
1 celery stick, sliced diagonally
1 leek, finely sliced
1 red pepper, cut into strips
1 small can bamboo shoots, sliced
140ml/¼ pint chicken, or other light stock
30g/1oz peas
1 tsp cornflour
1 tbsp water
Salt and pepper

1. Soak the noodles in hot water for 8 minutes, or as directed on the packet. Rinse in cold water and drain thoroughly.

2. Combine the wine, soy sauce and sugar in a large bowl. Add the pork, mix together well, and set aside to marinate for at least 15 minutes.

3. Heat the oil in a large wok, and add the ginger, celery and leek. Stir-fry for 2 minutes.

4. Add the red pepper and bamboo shoots to the wok, and stir-fry for a further 2 minutes.

5. Remove the vegetables from the wok. Increase the heat and add the pork, reserving the marinade. Stir-fry the pork over a high heat for 4 minutes, or until cooked through.

6. Return the vegetables to the wok, mixing with the pork. Add the chicken stock gradually, stirring well between additions.

7. Add the peas and cook for 2 minutes.

8. Mix the cornflour to a smooth paste with the water. Add this to the marinade and stir in well.

9. Stir the marinade into the vegetables and pork in the wok. Mix well, until the sauce is evenly distributed and is thickened and smooth. Add the noodles and stir everything together thoroughly until it has heated through.

10. Season to taste and simmer for 3 minutes before serving.

TIME: Preparation takes about 25 minutes including marinating time, and cooking takes about 20 minutes.

VARIATIONS: Substitute sliced beef or chicken for the pork.

SERVING IDEAS: Serve with plain boiled rice and prawn crackers.

LESCO

A popular recipe from Hungary that makes a very quick and tasty meal.

SERVES 4-6

---

2 medium green peppers
2 medium yellow peppers
1 large onion, finely sliced
2-3 tbsps sunflower oil
2 tbsps paprika
3 medium tomatoes, skinned and quartered
2 eggs, well beaten
Cooked rice, to serve

1. Cut the peppers into strips.

2. Heat a wok and fry the onion in the oil for 1-2 minutes, until just coloured.

3. Add the paprika, and stir well.

4. Add the peppers and stir-fry for about 2 minutes.

5. Add the tomatoes and stir-fry for a further minute.

6. Add the beaten eggs and seasoning.

7. Stir well until just cooked.

8. Serve immediately on a bed of rice.

TIME: Preparation takes 10 minutes, cooking takes about 10 minutes.

SERVING IDEAS: Lesco can be served with boiled potatoes instead of rice.

VARIATIONS: Red peppers may be used in place of the yellow peppers.

STIR-FRIED CALVES' LIVER WITH PEPPERS AND CARROTS

Calves' liver is a little more expensive than other types of liver, but is so delicious and nutritious, that it should be used more frequently.

SERVES 4

2 tbsps olive oil
1 onion, thinly sliced
1 clove garlic, cut into very thin strips
600g/1¼lb calves' liver, cut into thin strips
2 tbsps seasoned flour
60ml/4 tbsps dry sherry
140ml/¼ pint water, or vegetable stock
1 green pepper, cut into thin strips
3 large carrots, cut into strips
Freshly ground sea salt and black pepper,
    to taste
120g/4oz bean sprouts

1. Heat the olive oil in a wok. Add the onion and garlic, and stir-fry for 3 minutes.

2. Roll the strips of liver in the seasoned flour and add them to the wok, along with the onion. Stir-fry quickly, until the liver is sealed on the outside, but is still pink in the centre.

3. Stir the sherry into the liver, and bring to a rapid boil. Add the water, or stock, to the liver, along with the green pepper, carrots and seasoning to taste.

4. Stir-fry the liver in the sauce for 3 minutes, over a high heat.

5. Add the bean sprouts to the wok and stir-fry for 1 minute, or just long enough to heat the bean sprouts through without softening them.

TIME: Preparation takes 15-20 minutes, and cooking takes 10-12 minutes.

VARIATIONS: Use lambs' or pigs' liver for a stronger flavour.

SERVING IDEAS: Serve with a bowl of brown rice and a tasty tomato salad.

BEEF WITH ONIONS

*Marinated beef, sautéed with onions, garlic and ginger and served in
a smooth sauce.*

SERVES 4

450g/1lb fillet steak
2 tbsps oil
1 tsp sesame oil
1 tbsp Chinese wine
1 piece fresh ginger root, peeled and
   roughly chopped
3 onions, finely sliced
1 garlic clove, chopped
280ml/½ pint beef stock
1 pinch of sugar
2 tbsps dark soy sauce
1 tsp cornflour, combined with a little water
Salt and pepper

1. Cut the fillet into very thin slices.

2. Mix together half the oil, the sesame oil and wine and stir in the meat. Leave to marinate for 30 minutes.

3. Heat the remaining oil in a wok and stir-fry the ginger, onions and garlic until lightly browned.

4. Lift the meat out of the marinade with a slotted spoon and discard the marinade. Add the meat to the wok and stir-fry with the vegetables.

5. Pour over the stock, sugar and soy sauce. Cook for 4 minutes.

6. Thicken the sauce with the cornflour, stirring continuously until the desired consistency is reached. Season with salt and pepper and serve immediately.

TIME: Preparation takes about 15 minutes, plus 30 minutes marinating, and cooking takes approximately 20 minutes.

SERVING IDEAS: Serve this dish on a bed of boiled or steamed white rice.

SWEET AND SOUR PORK AND PINEAPPLE

A classic Chinese recipe that is easy to prepare at home.

SERVES 4

450g/1lb lean pork fillet, cut into 2.5cm/
    1-inch cubes
2 tbsps light soy sauce
2 tbsps white wine vinegar
2 tbsps tomato purée
1 tbsp sugar
2 tbsps peanut oil
1 tbsp cornflour
1 clove garlic, crushed
1 tsp grated root ginger
140ml/¼ pint water
1 can pineapple pieces, drained
Fresh coriander to garnish

1. Place the pork in bowl, pour over light soy sauce and toss together. Leave to marinate for 15 minutes.

2. Meanwhile, make the sauce, by mixing together the vinegar, tomato purée and sugar, and set aside.

3. Heat a wok and add the oil.

4. Remove pork from soy sauce, and add soy sauce to sauce mixture. Toss pork in cornflour, coating well.

5. When oil is hot, brown pork well all over. Remove from pan and reduce heat.

6. Fry garlic and ginger for 30 seconds. Add water. Bring to the boil, then return pork to wok.

7. Reduce heat; cover and simmer for 15 minutes, stirring occasionally.

8. Add sauce mixture and pineapple, and simmer for a further 15 minutes. Garnish with coriander.

TIME: Preparation takes 15 minutes and cooking takes about 20 minutes.

WATCHPOINT: Take care when you add the water to the wok.

SERVING IDEAS: Serve with rice and prawn crackers.

BEEF WITH TOMATO & PEPPER IN BLACK BEAN SAUCE

Black beans are a speciality of Cantonese cooking and give a pungent, salty taste to stir-fried dishes.

SERVES 6

2 large tomatoes
2 tbsps salted black beans
2 tbsps water
60ml/4 tbsps dark soy sauce
1 tbsp cornflour
1 tbsp dry sherry
1 tsp sugar
450g/1lb rump steak, cut into thin strips
1 small green pepper
60ml/4 tbsps oil
175ml/6 fl oz beef stock
Pinch ground black pepper

1. Core tomatoes and cut them into 16 wedges. Crush the black beans, add the water and set aside.

2. Combine soy sauce, cornflour, sherry, sugar and meat in a bowl and set aside.

3. Cut pepper into 1.25cm/½-inch diagonal pieces. Heat the wok and add the oil. When hot, stir-fry the green pepper pieces for about 1 minute and remove.

4. Add the meat and the soy sauce mixture to the wok and stir-fry for about 2 minutes. Add the soaked black beans and the stock. Bring to the boil and allow to thicken slightly.

5. Return the peppers to the wok and add the tomatoes and black pepper. Heat through for 1 minute and serve immediately.

TIME: Preparation takes about 25 minutes, cooking takes about 5 minutes.

SERVING IDEAS: Serve with plain boiled rice.

WATCHPOINT: Do not add the tomatoes too early or stir the mixture too vigorously once they are added or they will fall apart easily.

VARIATIONS: Substitute mange tout for the green peppers in the recipe. Mushrooms may also be added and cooked with the peppers or mange tout.

DUCK WITH ORANGE

Duck is quite a rich meat and is complemented perfectly by the tang of orange.

SERVES 4

3 oranges
1 small duck
1 tbsp oil
15g/½oz butter or margarine
280ml/½ pint light chicken stock
90ml/3 fl oz red wine
2 tbsps redcurrant jelly
Salt and pepper
1 tsp arrowroot
1 tbsp cold water
Watercress to garnish

1. Thinly pare the rind from 2 oranges and cut into fine shreds. Blanch in hot water and set aside for garnish.

2. Extract the juice from 2 oranges. Cut peel and pith from 1 orange, and then slice the flesh into rounds, or cut into segments if preferred.

3. Wash duck and dry well with kitchen paper.

4. Heat a wok, and add the oil and butter. When hot, add duck, and brown all over.

5. Remove from wok and, using poultry shears or a chopper, cut the duck in half lengthways, and then cut each half into 2.5cm/1-inch strips.

6. Return duck to wok, and add stock, red wine, redcurrant jelly, orange juice and rind, and salt and pepper to taste. Bring to boil, reduce heat, cover and simmer gently for 20 minutes.

7. Add orange slices, and simmer a further 10 minutes, or until duck is cooked.

8. If the sauce needs to be thickened, mix arrowroot with cold water and add to sauce.

9. Bring to the boil, and simmer for 3 minutes.

10. Garnish with reserved shreds of orange peel and watercress.

TIME: Preparation takes 30 minutes and cooking takes about 50 minutes.

COOK'S TIP: This dish is probably easiest eaten with the fingers, so set finger bowls of cold water with sliced lemon on the table.

VARIATION: Try using pork spare ribs instead of the duck.

FRIED RICE

A basic recipe for a traditional Chinese accompaniment to stir-fried dishes, this can be more substantial with the addition of meat, poultry or seafood.

SERVES 6-8

3 tbsps oil
1 egg, beaten
1 tbsp soy sauce
450g/1lb cooked rice, well drained and
    dried
60g/2oz cooked peas
Salt and pepper
Dash sesame oil
2 spring onions, thinly sliced

1. Heat a wok and add the oil. Pour in the egg and soy sauce and cook until just beginning to set.

2. Add the rice and peas and stir to coat with the egg mixture. Allow to cook for about 3 minutes, stirring continuously. Add seasoning and sesame oil.

3. Spoon into a serving dish and sprinkle over the spring onions.

TIME: The rice will take about 15 minutes to cook. Allow at least 20 minutes for it to drain as dry as possible. The fried rice dish will take about 4 minutes to cook.

VARIATIONS: Cooked meat, poultry or seafood may be added to the rice along with the peas.

COOK'S TIP: The 450g/1lb rice measurement is the cooked weight.

SPICY ORIENTAL NOODLES

A most versatile vegetable dish, this goes well with meat or stands alone for a vegetarian main course.

SERVES 4

225g/8oz Chinese noodles (medium thickness)
75ml/5 tbsps oil
4 carrots
225g/8oz broccoli
12 dried Chinese shiitake mushrooms, soaked 20 minutes in boiling water
4 spring onions, diagonally sliced
1 clove garlic, peeled
1-2 tsps chilli sauce, mild or hot
60ml/4 tbsps soy sauce
60ml/4 tbsps rice wine or dry sherry
2 tsps cornflour

1. Cook noodles in boiling, salted water for about 4-5 minutes. Drain well, rinse under hot water to remove starch and drain again. Toss with about 1 tbsp of the oil to prevent sticking.

2. Slice the carrots thinly on the diagonal.

3. Cut the broccoli florets off the stems and divide into even-sized but not too small sections. Slice the stalks thinly on the diagonal. If they seem tough, peel them before slicing.

4. Place the vegetables in boiling water for about 2 minutes to blanch. Drain and rinse under cold water to stop the cooking, and leave to drain dry.

5. Remove and discard the mushroom stems and slice the caps thinly. Set aside with the spring onions.

6. Heat a wok and add the remaining oil with the garlic clove. Leave the garlic in the pan while the oil heats and then remove it. Add the carrots and broccoli and stir-fry about 1 minute. Add mushrooms and spring onions and continue to stir-fry, tossing the vegetables in the pan continuously.

7. Combine chilli sauce, soy sauce, wine and cornflour, mixing well. Pour over the vegetables and cook, stirring, until the sauce clears. Toss with the noodles, heat them through and serve immediately.

TIME: Preparation takes about 20 minutes including soaking time, and cooking takes about 7-8 minutes.

BUYING GUIDE: Dried shiitake mushrooms are available at Oriental stores. Some large supermarkets now sell fresh shiitake which can be used instead, and need no soaking.

SERVING IDEAS: Use as a side dish with chicken, meat or fish, or serve as a starter. May also be served cold as a salad.

THE BUDDHIST'S DELIGHT

This vegetable side dish uses some ingredients which can be found at Oriental supermarkets.

SERVES 4

60g/2oz 'black moss' or 'hair' seaweed
8 dried Chinese mushrooms
15g/½oz bean curd skin (optional)
6 water chestnuts, sliced
225g/8oz Chinese cabbage, shredded
3 tbsps pine nuts
1 carrot, sliced
250ml/8 fl oz vegetable or chicken stock
1 tsp salt
1½ tbsps light soy sauce
2 tbsps oil
1 tbsp cornflour
3 tbsps water
1 tsp sesame oil

1. Soak the seaweed in boiling water for 40 minutes; the mushrooms for 10 minutes; and the bean curd skin for 5 minutes. Drain, then slice the mushrooms and bean curd skin.

2. Place all the ingredients, except the cornflour, water and sesame oil, in a wok and bring to the boil. Reduce the heat and simmer for 5 minutes.

3. Blend the cornflour with the water and add to the wok with the sesame oil. Bring to the boil, stirring, and simmer for 2 minutes.

TIME: Preparation takes 45 minutes and cooking takes 8-10 minutes.

BUYING GUIDE: Fresh Chinese shiitake mushrooms can now be bought at many large supermarkets, and need no soaking.

PRAWN EGG RICE

Serve this on its own for a tasty lunch or supper dish, or as part of a more elaborate Chinese meal.

SERVES 6

450g/1lb long grain rice
2 eggs
½ tsp salt
60ml/4 tbsps oil
1 large onion, chopped
2 cloves of garlic, chopped
120g/4oz peeled prawns
60g/2oz frozen peas
2 spring onions, chopped
2 tbsps dark soy sauce

1. Wash the rice thoroughly and put it in a wok. Add water to come 2.5cm/1 inch above the top of the rice.

2. Bring the rice to the boil, stir once, then reduce the heat. Cover and simmer the rice for 5-7 minutes, or until the liquid has been absorbed.

3. Rinse the rice in cold water and fluff up with a fork, to separate the grains.

4. Beat the eggs with a pinch of salt. Heat 1 tbsp of the oil in the wok and cook the onion until soft, but not brown. Pour in the egg and stir gently, until the mixture is set. Remove the egg mixture and set it aside.

5. Heat a further tablespoon of the oil and fry the garlic, prawns, peas and spring onions quickly for 2 minutes. Remove from the wok and set aside.

6. Heat the remaining oil in the wok and stir in the rice and remaining salt. Stir-fry, to heat the rice through, then add the egg and the prawn mixtures and the soy sauce, stirring to blend thoroughly. Serve immediately.

TIME: Preparation takes about 20 minutes and cooking takes about 15 minutes.

VARIATIONS: Use chopped red peppers or corn kernels, instead of the peas.

TO FREEZE: Rice can be cooked and frozen for up to 6 weeks. Frozen rice should be defrosted and rinsed, before being used in this dish.

VEGETABLE CHOP SUEY

Stir-fried vegetables should still be slightly crisp when cooked correctly and so add texture as well as flavour to the meal.

SERVES 4

1 green pepper, seeded
1 red pepper, seeded
1 carrot
½ cucumber
1 courgette, thickly peeled and the central core discarded
1 onion
2 cloves garlic
2 tbsps oil
2 tsps sugar
2 tbsps soy sauce
120ml/4 fl oz chicken stock
Salt and pepper

1. Cut all the vegetables into thin slices, use only the outside of the courgette. Prepare the onion by slicing it in half, then in quarters, and finally in thin, even slices.

2. Chop the garlic very finely.

3. Heat the oil in a wok and stir-fry the peppers and garlic for 30 seconds.

4. Add the onion and the carrot and stir-fry for a further 30 seconds.

5. Add the cucumber and the courgette, cook for a further 1 minute, stirring and shaking the wok continuously.

6. Stir in the sugar, soy sauce, chicken stock, salt and pepper, mixing together evenly. Simmer until all the ingredients are fully incorporated. Serve piping hot.

TIME: Preparation takes about 15 minutes and cooking takes approximately 5 minutes.

VARIATION: You could add blanched bean sprouts or sliced, blanched bamboo shoots to this dish.

COOK'S TIP: If you follow the order given above for cooking the vegetables, they will all be cooked but still slightly crisp.

GADO GADO

This makes a very appealing side dish for a dinner party based on Chinese or Indonesian dishes.

SERVES 4

1 tbsp peanut oil
1 carrot, cut into thin strips
1 potato, cut into thin strips
120g/4oz green beans, trimmed
120g/4oz Chinese cabbage, shredded
120g/4oz beansprouts
Half a cucumber, cut into batons

Peanut Sauce
2 tbsps peanut oil
60g/2oz raw shelled peanuts
2 red chillies, deseeded and finely
    chopped, or 1 tsp chilli powder
2 shallots, finely chopped
1 clove garlic, crushed
140ml/¼ pint water
1 tsp brown sugar
Juice of ½ a lemon
Salt
90ml/3 fl oz coconut milk
Sliced hard-boiled eggs, to garnish
Sliced cucumber, to garnish

1. Heat a wok and add 1 tbsp peanut oil. When hot, toss in the carrot and potato. Stir-fry for 2 minutes and add green beans and cabbage. Cook for a further 3 minutes.

2. Add the beansprouts and cucumber, and stir-fry for 2 minutes.

3. Place in a serving dish and keep warm.

4. Make the peanut sauce. Heat the wok, add the 2 tbsps peanut oil, and fry the peanuts for 2-3 minutes. Remove and drain on kitchen paper.

5. Blend or pound chillies, shallots and garlic to a smooth paste. Grind or blend peanuts to a powder.

6. Reheat oil and fry the chilli paste for 2 minutes.

7. Add the water, and bring to the boil. Add peanuts, brown sugar, lemon juice, and salt to taste. Stir until sauce is thick – about 10 minutes – and add coconut milk.

8. Garnish vegetable dish with slices of hard-boiled egg and cucumber, and serve with the peanut sauce.

TIME: Preparation takes about 20 minutes and cooking takes 30 minutes.

SERVING IDEAS: This dish could also be served as a vegetarian main course for two people.

COOK'S TIP: Make sure that all the vegetables and garnish are prepared before you start cooking this dish.

SPAGHETTI RICE

*This **unusual** combination of pasta and rice makes a deliciously different side dish.*

SERVES 4

120g/4oz uncooked long grain rice
120g/4oz uncooked spaghetti, broken into
    5cm/2-inch pieces
3 tbsps oil
60ml/4 tbsps sesame seeds
2 tbsps chopped chives
Salt and pepper
430ml/¾ pint chicken, beef or vegetable
    stock
1 tbsp soy sauce
2 tbsps chopped parsley

1. Rinse the rice and pasta to remove starch, and leave to drain dry.

2. Heat the oil in a large wok and add the dried rice and pasta. Cook over moderate heat to brown the rice and pasta, stirring continuously.

3. Add the sesame seeds and cook until the rice, pasta and seeds are golden brown.

4. Add the chives, salt and pepper, and pour over 280ml/½ pint stock. Stir in the soy sauce and bring to the boil.

5. Cover and cook for about 20 minutes, or until the rice and pasta are tender and the stock is absorbed. Add more of the reserved stock as necessary. Do not let the rice and pasta dry out during cooking.

6. Fluff up the grains of rice with a fork and sprinkle with the parsley before serving.

TIME: Preparation takes about 25 minutes and cooking takes about
20 minutes or more.

VARIATIONS: Use other herbs, or spring onions instead of chives to flavour
this dish.

SERVING IDEAS: Serve as a side dish with meat or poultry. Give it an
Italian flavour by omitting sesame seeds, chives and soy sauce and
substituting Parmesan and basil instead.

SPECIAL MIXED VEGETABLES

This dish illustrates the basic stir-frying technique for vegetables. Use other varieties for an equally colourful side dish.

SERVES 4

3 tomatoes
1 tbsp oil
1 clove garlic, crushed
2.5cm/1-inch piece fresh root ginger, sliced
4 Chinese leaves, shredded
60g/2oz flat mushrooms, thinly sliced
60g/2oz bamboo shoots, sliced
3 celery sticks, diagonally sliced
60g/2oz baby corn, cut in half if large
1 small red pepper, thinly sliced
60g/2oz bean sprouts
2 tbsps light soy sauce
Dash sesame oil
Salt and pepper

1. To make it easier to skin the tomatoes, remove the stems and place in boiling water for 5 seconds.

2. Remove from the boiling water with a draining spoon and place in cold water. This will make the skins easier to remove. Cut out the core end using a small sharp knife.

3. Cut the tomatoes in half and then core and quarter them. Use a teaspoon or a serrated edged knife to remove the seeds.

4. Heat the oil in a wok and add all the vetegables, apart from the tomatoes, in the order given.

5. Cook the vegetables for about 2 minutes. Stir in the soy sauce, sesame oil, salt and pepper and add the tomatoes. Heat through for 30 seconds and serve immediately.

TIME: Preparation takes about 25 minutes, cooking takes about 2½-3 minutes.

VARIATIONS: Other vegetables such as broccoli florets, cauliflower florets, mange tout, courgettes or French beans may be used.

SERVING IDEAS: Serve as a side dish or as a vegetarian main course with plain or fried rice.

RICE AND BEAN PILAFF

A lively side dish or vegetarian main course, this recipe readily takes to creative variations and even makes a good cold salad.

SERVES 6-8

60ml/4 tbsps oil
225g/8oz long grain rice
1 onion, finely chopped
1 green pepper, chopped
1 tsp each ground cumin and coriander
Dash Tabasco sauce
Salt
1 litre/1¾ pints vegetable stock
450g/1lb canned red kidney beans, drained and rinsed
450g/1lb canned tomatoes, drained and coarsely chopped
Chopped parsley

1. Heat the oil in a wok.

2. Add the rice and cook until just turning opaque. Add the onion, pepper and cumin and coriander. Cook gently for a further 2 minutes.

3. Add the Tabasco, salt, stock and beans and bring to the boil. Cover and cook about 45 minutes, or until the rice is tender and most of the liquid is absorbed.

4. Remove from the heat and add the tomatoes, stirring them in gently. Leave to stand, covered, for 5 minutes.

5. Fluff up the mixture with a fork and sprinkle with parsley to serve.

TIME: Preparation takes about 25 minutes and cooking takes about 50 minutes.

SERVING IDEAS: Serve with bread and a salad for a light vegetarian meal. Serve as a side dish with meat or poultry, or cheese and egg dishes.

VARIATIONS: The recipe may be made with 450g/1lb fresh tomatoes, skinned, seeded and coarsely chopped.

OKRA AND TOMATOES

Okra, also known as ladies fingers, is a common ingredient in Indian cooking and blends well with a variety of spices.

SERVES 4

---

1 tbsp oil or ghee
¼ tsp turmeric
¼ tsp chilli powder
½ tsp garam masala
1 onion, chopped
225g/8oz okra, sliced into 1.5cm/½-inch pieces
1 red chilli, seeded and finely sliced
2 tomatoes, chopped
140ml/¼ pint water
Salt

1. Heat a wok and add the oil or ghee. When hot, add the turmeric, chilli powder and garam masala, and stir-fry for 30 seconds.

2. Add the onion, okra and red chilli, and stir-fry for 3 minutes.

3. Add the tomatoes, water, and salt to taste, and cook uncovered for 5 minutes or until the sauce thickens.

TIME: Preparation takes 15 minutes and cooking takes 10 minutes.

COOK'S TIP: When okra are cut up they become gluey during cooking. To cook them on their own just trim off stalks and cook whole.

BUYING GUIDE: Okra are available in some large supermarkets and Oriental stores.

NOODLES WITH GINGER AND OYSTER SAUCE

Noodles stir-fried with ginger, carrot and courgettes, then served in an oyster sauce.

SERVES 4

225g/8oz Chinese noodles
1 carrot
1 courgette
3 slices fresh root ginger
1 tbsp oil
1 spring onion, cut into thin rounds
1 tbsp soy sauce
2 tbsps oyster sauce
Salt and pepper

---

1. Cook the noodles in boiling, salted water, rinse them under cold water, and set aside to drain.

2. Cut the carrot into thin strips. Thickly peel the courgette to include a little of the flesh and cut into thin strips. Discard the centre of the courgette.

3. Peel the ginger sparingly, but remove any hard parts. Slice thinly, using a potato peeler. Cut the slices into thin strips, using a very sharp knife.

4. Heat the oil in a wok, and stir-fry the spring onion for 10 seconds; add the carrot, courgette and ginger, and stir-fry briefly.

5. Stir in the noodles and cook for 1 minute.

6. Stir in the soy sauce and oyster sauces and continue cooking until heated through. Season with salt and pepper and serve.

TIME: Preparation takes about 15 minutes and cooking takes approximately 15 minutes.

VARIATION: Cook the noodles in chicken stock instead of salted water to give them extra flavour.

COOK'S TIP: Stir-fry the ginger and the other vegetables very quickly, to avoid browning them. Lower the heat if necessary.

STIR-FRIED VEGETABLE MEDLEY

Stir-frying is a very good method of cooking vegetables as it is so brief. When cooked the vegetables should still be slightly crunchy.

SERVES 4

2 carrots
225g/8oz broccoli
1 onion
1 courgette
2 celery sticks
2 tbsps oil
¼ tsp finely grated fresh root ginger
1 clove garlic, crushed
1 can baby sweetcorn, drained
1 tbsp light soy sauce
Salt and pepper

1. Cut the carrots into flowers by cutting out 5 small V-shaped grooves lengthwise around the carrots. Cut carrots crosswise into rounds.

2. Divide broccoli into small florets and slit the stems to ensure quick cooking.

3. Slice onion into julienne strips.

4. Diagonally slice the courgette and celery.

5. Heat a wok and add the oil. Add ginger, garlic, onion, carrots, broccoli and courgette, and toss in oil for 2-3 minutes.

6. Add the celery and baby sweetcorn, and toss 1-2 minutes longer.

7. Season with soy sauce, and salt and pepper if wished.

TIME: Preparation takes about 20 minutes and cooking takes 4-5 minutes.

PREPARATION: Make sure that you prepare all the ingredients before starting to cook this dish.

COOK'S TIP: Add some cornflour, blended with a little water, to thicken the vegetable juices if necessary.

PEKING TOFFEE APPLES

A quick and easy dessert to prepare and one which you never grow out of!

SERVES 4

4 crisp apples
1 egg
60g/2oz flour
Oil for deep frying
90g/6 tbsps sugar
3 tbsps oil
3 tbsps golden syrup

1. Peel, core and thickly slice the apples.

2. Blend the egg, flour and 60ml/4 tbsps water to make a smooth batter.

3. Place oil for deep frying in a wok and heat to a moderate temperature, about 180°C/350°F.

4. Dip the apple slices in the batter just before frying.

5. Deep-fry the apple, several slices at a time, for 2-3 minutes or until golden. Drain on kitchen paper and keep warm.

6. Heat the sugar, oil and 2 tbsps water in a pan over a low heat, until the sugar dissolves. Turn up the heat and cook for about 5 minutes until the sugar starts to caramelise. Stir in the syrup and heat for a further 2 minutes.

7. Add the apple pieces and stir slowly, covering each piece of apple with syrup.

8. Quickly spoon hot, syrup-covered apples into a large bowl of iced water to harden syrup. Remove quickly and serve.

TIME: Preparation takes 10 minutes, cooking takes 10 minutes.

PREPARATION: Only coat the apples with batter as you fry them or they will become soggy if left to stand.

WATCHPOINT: Make sure you keep an eye on the sugar as it caramelises to ensure that it doesn't burn.

105

BANANAS COOKED IN COCONUT MILK

A very simple dish to prepare and especially popular with children.

SERVES 4

---

1 tbsp brown sugar
120g/4oz desiccated coconut
430ml/¾ pint milk
4-6 large, ripe bananas, peeled and sliced
    diagonally into 3 or 4 pieces
Desiccated coconut to decorate

1. Put the sugar, coconut and milk into a wok, and bring to simmering point. Turn off heat and allow to cool for 15 minutes.

2. Push through a sieve or a piece of muslin to squeeze out juices.

3. Return to the wok, and simmer for 10 minutes, or until creamy.

4. Add the bananas and cook slowly until they are soft.

5. Serve immediately sprinkled with desiccated coconut.

TIME: Preparation takes about 20 minutes and cooking takes 20 minutes.

PREPARATION: Substitute 4 tbsp canned coconut milk or 2 tbsp instant, powdered coconut milk for the desiccated coconut. Preparation is quicker, just bring to simmering then continue from Step 3.

BUYING GUIDE: Canned coconut milk is available in Oriental stores and large supermarkets. Instant, powdered coconut milk is now available in some large supermarkets.

FRUIT TURNOVERS

Use bought shortcrust pastry, either fresh or frozen and defrosted
to make this recipe easy.

MAKES 10

450g/1lb shortcrust pastry
Oil for deep frying
10 ripe fresh apricots, halved and stoned, or
    450g/1lb canned apricots, well drained
450g/1lb cream cheese
Icing sugar

1. Roll out pastry and cut into 10 even sized rounds. Heat oil in a wok to a depth of at least 5cm/2 inches. Oil should reach a temperature of 190°C/375°F.

2. Cut the apricots into quarters and the cheese into 10 even pieces.

3. Place one piece of cheese and an even amount of apricots on the lower half of each pastry round. Fold over the upper half and seal the edges. Crimp tightly into a decorative pattern.

4. Fry one turnover at a time until golden on both sides. Baste the upper side frequently with oil.

5. Drain well on kitchen paper and serve warm, sprinkled with icing sugar.

TIME: Preparation takes about 20 minutes and cooking takes about 45 minutes.

VARIATIONS: Other fruit may be used in the turnovers instead of apricots. Substitute fresh guava, mango or papaya cut into short strips. Sliced peaches may also be used as well as cherries.

PREPARATION: As with all deep-fried foods, these turnovers are best served as soon as they are cooked.

SWEET BEAN WONTONS

Wonton snacks, either sweet or savoury, are a popular tea house treat in China. Made from prepared wonton wrappers and ready-made bean paste, these couldn't be more simple.

SERVES 6

15 wonton wrappers
225g/8oz sweet red bean paste
1 tbsp cornflour
60ml/4 tbsps cold water
Oil for deep frying
Honey

1. Take a wonton wrapper in the palm of your hand and place a little of the red bean paste slightly above the centre.

2. Mix together the cornflour and water and moisten the edge around the filling.

3. Fold over diagonally, slightly off centre.

4. Pull the sides together, using the cornflour and water paste to stick the two together.

5. Turn inside out by gently pushing the filled centre through the middle.

6. Heat enough oil in a wok for deep-fat frying and when hot, put in 4 of the filled wontons at a time. Cook until crisp and golden and remove to kitchen paper to drain. Repeat with the remaining filled wontons. Serve drizzled with honey.

TIME: Preparation takes about 20 minutes, cooking takes about 20 minutes in total.

VARIATIONS: Add a small amount of grated ginger to the red bean paste for a slight change in flavour. Wontons may also be sprinkled with sugar instead of honey.

BUYING GUIDE: Wonton wrappers and red bean paste are available in Chinese supermarkets.

Index